J. WESTON
WALCH
PUBLISHER

100 Writing Starters
for Middle School

Ann Bourman

User's Guide
to
Walch Reproducible Books

Purchasers of this book are granted the right to reproduce all pages where this symbol appears:

This permission is limited to a single teacher, for classroom use only.

Any questions regarding this policy or requests to purchase further reproduction rights should be addressed to:

Permissions Editor
J. Weston Walch, Publisher
321 Valley Street • P.O. Box 658
Portland, Maine 04104-0658

ISBN 0-8251-4350-0
Copyright © 1991, 2002
J. Weston Walch, Publisher
www.walch.com
Printed in the United States of America

Wieser Educational

30281 Esperanza
Rancho Santa Margarita, CA 92688-2130
1(800) 880-4433 ♦ Fax (800) 949-0209

www.wieser-ed.com ♦ Email info@wieser-ed.com

Contents

To the Teacher

These writing-starter exercises are designed to be used for practice in paragraph writing and in simple expository writing. They were written for the middle school and junior high school grades, but they may be used in upper elementary grades or senior high school classes if you find that they are suitable for your particular students.

Students write best if they write from their own experiences, and these paragraphs provide that opportunity. Each page has a paragraph on a subject with which most middle school students will be familiar.

Students also write well if they are first guided through a very structured exercise. Here, they are given a beginning. They must provide a continuation and an ending. Later, they can begin as well as complete their own paragraphs and short compositions.

The first paragraph on each page is four or five sentences long. Then the opening sentence of the second paragraph is given. The first word of the second sentence is also given. Students are to continue writing from this first word of the second sentence and complete the paragraph. They should have a total of five sentences in the second paragraph when they are done. (This total includes the first printed sentence.)

There is nothing magic about the numbers of sentences used in the exercises. These numbers are used because they seem to yield exercises short enough not to intimidate the unpracticed writer, but long enough to allow for some substance.

It would be best to reproduce a page for each student and allow him or her to write directly on the reproduced copy. This form of presentation should help students go right into writing a continuation that "flows" from what they are given.

No slackers or shortcuts allowed! Do not accept a paper to which the student has added only a sentence or two. Five full sentences in the second paragraph, including the one given, are required.

The first time you use these exercises, you may want to read the two completed samples to the class. Show them that by the time they get to the final sentence, the ideas have also come to a conclusion. This necessity for a concluding thought is illustrated in the samples given. You can complete others yourself as samples, if that would be useful. You may want to post several samples on the bulletin board and allow students to look at them as they are working on their own papers.

Use these exercises wherever and whenever they fit into your own writing lessons.

Variations

1. Give copies of the *same* page to all members of the class. After they write, have a number of students read their papers aloud. Point out the variety of responses created by different authors.

2. Give copies of *different* pages to all members of the class. After they write, have a number of students read their papers aloud. Discuss each paper in terms of logical continuation and ending, as well as clarity of writing.

3. Have copies of *different* pages available to students to use for "extra credit" when they are finished with other class assignments. Students may select the ones they want to do from your stack of reproduced copies. (These exercises are a good length for moments that need to be filled; they also can be done on an individual basis, and there is a wide choice of topics.)

4. Use these exercises as class "openers." They can be done in just a few minutes, so they can be used as an opening exercise in a class period to focus student attention and to get them quiet and working. You could then collect the exercises and assign written grades.

Grading Tip

Students should write frequently, which means that English teachers are often buried in grading and paperwork. Let students know that one of every three (or five, or any number) of these exercises will be read word for word and assigned a grade. Decide whether you or the student will select the exercise(s) to be graded, according to what suits your classes best.

The result, we hope, will be a maximum amount of student writing with a reasonable amount of teacher reading and grading.

SAMPLE

Name_____ Date _____

36. I Can See Clearly Now

Ann was upset that the eye doctor had told her she needed to wear glasses. She would look awful in glasses! Her mother helped her pick some very pretty, stylish frames, but she still didn't like the idea. People might make fun of how she looked!

The first day Ann had the glasses, she was surprised to see how clear everything looked on the chalkboard. She . . .

could see all her friends very clearly and could read all the titles on the bulletin board way in the back of the room. The girl next to her told her that her glasses were cute. A boy at the next table asked her about the classwork without even mentioning her new glasses. Glasses might not be so bad after all!

NAME_____ DATE _____

90.   Surprise!

Isabel could not understand why her two closest friends had not mentioned her birthday. The three girls always exchanged birthday gifts and cards and hugs. But today, when Isabel turned fifteen, neither friend had said a thing! Isabel walked into her house wondering why they had forgotten.

As she opened the front door, Isabel heard at least a dozen voices yell, "Surprise!" She . . .

saw her two closest friends and lots of other kids from school crowded into her living room. Balloons and other decorations were hung all around. A huge decorated cake, plates, and cups of punch were on the table. As her friends began to sing "Happy Birthday," Isabel could tell that this would be her greatest birthday ever!

1.   Late . . . Again!

Tom ran in the front door of the school just two minutes before the late bell was supposed to ring. Would he get to his class on time? Mrs. Miller was very strict about such things. Tom had been in trouble before for being late.

As Tom opened the door to his class, he heard the bell ring. He . . .

_____

_____

_____

_____

_____

_____

_____

_____

_____

2. Caught in the Act

Teresa had never cheated on a test in her life. She had studied the math lessons for the week, but she just did not understand the methods used to solve some of the problems. She tried to look at Mike's paper, but he had his hand over his work. She looked over her shoulder at Rosa's paper.

As Teresa turned back to her own paper, she saw the teacher staring at her. He . . .

_____

_____

_____

_____

_____

_____

_____

_____

_____

_____

3. No Cuts!

Bill laughed and joked as he cut into the front of the lunch line. "I'm first!" he yelled. He did this nearly every day, and all the kids were sick of it but had given up trying to stop him. Bill played and shoved other students as he waited to buy his lunch.

One girl decided to speak up about Bill's rude behavior. She . . .

_____

_____

_____

_____

_____

_____

_____

_____

_____

4.　History in Person!

When Aaron's history class studied the Civil Rights Movement of the 1960s, Aaron had a unique contribution to make. He told the teacher that his uncle had been one of the first African-American teenagers to enter an all-white high school. This group of black students had become nationally famous. Aaron asked the teacher if he should invite his uncle to talk to the class. The teacher responded with an enthusiastic "Yes!"

When Aaron's uncle came to the class several weeks later, many of the students were ready with questions. They . . .

_____

_____

_____

_____

_____

_____

_____

_____

_____

_____

5. Trouble in the Library

Mrs. Gill, the school librarian, was very helpful to students who came into the library to find books or to do research. She always suggested interesting books to read and good ways to begin a class assignment. She didn't even say "Shh!" too often! One day she was helping a boy in the reference center when she glanced up and saw a girl tearing a page out of a magazine that belonged to the library.

"That magazine is to be used here and not destroyed, young lady!" Mrs. Gill snapped. She . . .

_____

_____

_____

_____

_____

_____

_____

_____

6. We Want Daniel!

Mr. Porter, the school's music teacher, conducted the school band. He had been at the school for many years and did a good job, but he was thinking of retiring. One year he had a student teacher, Daniel, who brought new spirit to the band. When Daniel stood up to conduct, his energy and enthusiasm made the band members love him.

One day when Daniel could not come to band practice, Mr. Porter stood up to conduct, and the band members shouted that they wanted Daniel instead! Mr. Porter . . .

_____

_____

_____

_____

_____

_____

_____

_____

_____

7.   Hit and Run

On her way to her friend's house one Saturday afternoon, Maria saw a car accident. Luckily, no one was hurt, but she could see it was a hit-and-run accident. One driver had hit the side of the second car, dented it badly, and then driven off in a hurry.

Maria memorized the license number of the car as it sped away. She . . .

_____

_____

_____

_____

_____

_____

_____

_____

_____

_____

8. What to Say?

Mrs. Thomas felt sad when she read a composition by her eighth-grade English student, Luis. He wrote that he felt ugly and that no girl would ever like him. He even wrote that his parents told him he was handsome, but he claimed they just said that because they "had to" since they were his parents. Mrs. Thomas wanted to say something that would make Luis feel better about himself, but she could not decide what to say.

One day at lunchtime, Mrs. Thomas saw Luis sitting alone on a bench, so she walked over and sat down next to him. She . . .

_____

_____

_____

_____

_____

_____

_____

_____

9. A Forged Report Card

Jack knew his grades were going to be poor on his midterm report card and that his mother would punish him. So Jack used his computer to create a new report card, one that looked identical to the school's version. Instead of failing grades, he filled in excellent grades. Then he forged all the signatures in what he hoped looked like a variety of handwriting styles. Before his mother got home, he left the card on her desk, just as he always did.

When Jack's mother saw the card, she was immediately suspicious. She . . .

_____

_____

_____

_____

_____

_____

_____

_____

10. Proud to Be Me

Juan was tired of having other students make fun of his Spanish accent. He had come to the United States from Nicaragua just one year earlier, and he was proud of how well he had learned English. His family was proud of him, too, and often depended on him as a translator. Juan decided he would no longer ignore rude remarks about his speech or accent.

One afternoon in math class, a girl who made rude comments about many students loudly imitated Juan's accent. Juan . . .

_____

_____

_____

_____

_____

_____

_____

_____

_____

11.   Sorry, Cory!

All semester, Cory looked forward to the tryouts for graduation speakers. When they were held, he spoke confidently and felt he had done well. His friends told him he had sounded wonderful. A teacher remarked that he had received one of the highest scores of all the candidates.

But the next day, the class counselor told Cory that since he had a "fail" in his algebra class, he did not qualify for the ceremony at all and could not be a speaker. Cory . . .

_____

_____

_____

_____

_____

_____

_____

_____

12. Fight!

At the end of the lunch period, a fight broke out. Two girls who had been calling each other names began to hit each other. Then they pulled each other's hair and hit even more violently. Several friends of each girl tried to pull the fighters apart, but others in the crowd yelled at them to keep punching each other.

The school security guard stepped in and grabbed the girls in an effort to separate them. He . . .

_____

_____

_____

_____

_____

_____

_____

_____

_____

13. Richard's Wheels

Richard had been working and saving his money for over two years. He was ready to buy his first car! He had visited used car lots and had seen several cars he liked and could afford. He asked his father to come help him decide which would be the best. First Richard took him to see the bright red convertible with extra equipment, including a stereo.

Richard's father frowned when he first saw the car. He . . .

_____

_____

_____

_____

_____

_____

_____

_____

_____

14. Ivan at the Police Station

Ivan was usually very responsible, and he rarely got into trouble. When he went out with friends in the evening, he always came home on time. One Saturday night, however, Ivan was late. Just as Ivan's mother was starting to worry, the phone rang. "Mom, I'm at the police station!" Ivan exclaimed.

Ivan's mother was shocked. She . . .

_____

_____

_____

_____

_____

_____

_____

_____

_____

_____

15. Melody's Voice Is Heard!

In history class, Melody's teacher showed everyone how to compose and address a letter to the editor of the city newspaper. The students selected topics, wrote their letters, and addressed the envelopes. The teacher urged the students to mail the letters on their own. She even offered prizes to students whose letters were printed.

A week later, Melody saw that the teacher had taped that morning's editorial page to the chalkboard, and she saw her letter and name in print! She . . .

_____

_____

_____

_____

_____

_____

_____

_____

_____

16. Singled Out

Lian and several other students were asked to stay after class for a moment by their English teacher, Mrs. Page. Lian was surprised. Had she done something wrong? She began to feel nervous. When everyone else was gone, Mrs. Page told Lian and the other remaining students that she wanted to talk to them about something very important.

Lian leaned forward and listened carefully. Mrs. Page . . .

_____

_____

_____

_____

_____

_____

_____

_____

_____

17.   Alfred's Concert

When Alfred missed school for several weeks to travel to another state, his friends and teachers thought he had gone to visit relatives. When Alfred returned, he explained that he had been on a concert tour. At age thirteen, after seven years of study, he was a nearly professional pianist! "Alfred!" yelled a classmate. "Let's hear you play something!"

The whole class walked over to the music room, and Alfred sat down at the piano. He . . .

_____

_____

_____

_____

_____

_____

_____

_____

18. Tiffany's Trouble

Tiffany was one of the smartest students in the school. She earned top grades and had just been elected student body president. One day after school, her friends saw her sitting in the detention room, where students who had broken rules were required to "serve time." Her friends were amazed and could not imagine what in the world she might have done to deserve punishment.

The next morning, several girls met Tiffany at her locker and asked her why she had been in detention. She . . .

_____

_____

_____

_____

_____

_____

_____

_____

_____

19.   Unique Beauty

Sheryl was very pretty and unique in appearance. Her father was black and her mother was from Vietnam. She was proud of her background and felt great when she was told she was good-looking. Once in a while, however, comments were not so nice!

One morning a rather talkative and silly girl asked Sheryl, "Why are you so funny looking?" Sheryl . . .

_____

_____

_____

_____

_____

_____

_____

_____

_____

20. What's Wrong, Jeremy?

When Jeremy was in Mrs. Teeman's seventh-grade class, he was an A student and behaved well. In the eighth grade, he was in Mrs. Teeman's class again, but this time his grades dropped and he was not very cooperative. In fact, he was often very disruptive in class. Mrs. Teeman could not tell if she was seeing normal teenage changes or a problem.

Mrs. Teeman decided to have a meeting with Jeremy and his parents. She . . .

_____

_____

_____

_____

_____

_____

_____

_____

_____

21. Color Barrier

Susan walked across the school yard to have lunch with her friend Tanya. Susan was white and Tanya was black. Luckily, in their school, friendships between many different groups of people existed, and few students made prejudiced comments. On this day, however, one white girl stepped in front of Susan and Tanya, stared directly at Tanya, and yelled, "Why don't you stick with your own kind?"

Susan was so shocked she didn't quite know how to react, but she knew she had to do something. She . . .

_____

_____

_____

_____

_____

_____

_____

_____

22. Calling Mr. Sawyer

Mr. Sawyer, a substitute, was a poor teacher, even worse than the one the class had had a month before. He gave the day's assignment and then turned away from the class to read his newspaper! He offered no help at all with the day's work. He didn't seem to notice that most of the kids were shouting and playing instead of working.

Suddenly, a loud "bang" in the back of the class got Mr. Sawyer's attention. He . . .

_____

_____

_____

_____

_____

_____

_____

_____

23. Cute Nathan

Nathan checked into the school when the first quarter was half over. He was taller than most of the other boys, and so good-looking that all the girls couldn't help staring at him. He was quiet but friendly, with a great smile. Sheila saw her chance when the teacher announced that the next class project had to be done with a partner.

Sheila dashed across the room and asked Nathan if he'd like to work with her. Nathan . . .

_____

_____

_____

_____

_____

_____

_____

_____

_____

_____

24. Noisy Neighbors

The family that moved in next door to Kim seemed cheerful and friendly. The parents and two small children looked pleasant. Soon, however, the new family made constant, loud noise. Loud screaming between all the family members, a blasting television, and frequent door slamming seemed to go on nonstop.

Kim and her family could scarcely stand the noise, so Kim decided to do something. She . . .

_____

_____

_____

_____

_____

_____

_____

_____

_____

_____

25. Marieka's Stress

Marieka had practiced for weeks for the dance recital. She was very proud of her hard work and couldn't wait to perform for her friends and family. She had chosen a colorful costume and dynamic music. She imagined thunderous applause and a standing ovation! But the day of the recital, Marieka felt sick to her stomach. Her knees shook. Standing backstage, she watched the others perform their programs and thought about running out the exit.

Suddenly, Marieka was up! She . . .

_____

_____

_____

_____

_____

_____

_____

_____

_____

_____

_____

26. A Fair Grade?

Mrs. Reynolds was angry that her son Daryl had received a low grade in his history class. She was sure his teacher had graded him unfairly. She went to school and demanded that the teacher explain the grade and show evidence that it was accurate. She was loud and rude, and she embarrassed Daryl in front of the teacher and the principal.

The teacher calmly began to explain the grade. She . . .

_____

_____

_____

_____

_____

_____

_____

_____

_____

_____

27. Mi-Kyung Won!

Mi-Kyung, an immigrant from Korea, was already so skilled in English that she was the best writer in her creative writing class. Her papers were unusually thoughtful and mature for a thirteen-year-old student. When the teacher had all the class members enter a citywide writing contest, Mi-Kyung submitted a poem she had written. She hoped she would win first prize, a $100 savings bond.

About a month later, the teacher came to class waving a big envelope and cried out, "Mi-Kyung won first place in the poetry division!" Mi-Kyung . . .

_____

_____

_____

_____

_____

_____

_____

_____

28. Sound Battle

Each day after school, Tony listened to rock music and practiced playing his electric guitar. Each day, his mother called to him to turn the volume down. It was a continuing battle between the two of them. Tony insisted he had the volume low enough, and his mother insisted it was still too loud. Sometimes Tony got angry and yelled at his mother.

One day when Tony got home, his mother told him that he was not allowed to play the guitar in the house until he learned to be more respectful. Tony . . .

_____

_____

_____

_____

_____

_____

_____

_____

_____

29.   Earthquake!

One morning, just as the class had settled into their seats for the first lesson of the day, the room began to shake and the windows rattled. The teacher ordered the students to drop to the floor and face away from the windows, as they had many times during drills. This seemed to be the real thing!

As the room shook, Mandy burst into tears. She . . .

_____

_____

_____

_____

_____

_____

_____

_____

_____

30.   No Guns

For a term project in history class, students were asked to do research on famous individuals and then present their information in the form of plays or informal skits. Costumes and props were recommended to make the presentations interesting. The students looked forward to this entertaining way of presenting their information. During the first presentation, a student pulled out a toy gun as a prop because he represented a Western cowboy hero.

The class was surprised when the teacher interrupted the presentation, saying, "No guns!" She . . .

_____

_____

_____

_____

_____

_____

_____

_____

_____

31. Zachary's Secret

While cleaning his bedroom one afternoon, Zachary's mother found a marijuana cigarette and a small bag of the drug on the floor. She had not known her son had experimented with or used any drugs. She was very upset and wondered what she should do. She told herself to approach her son calmly, with no yelling or threats.

When Zachary came home, his mother asked him to sit down at the dining room table with her. She . . .

_____

_____

_____

_____

_____

_____

_____

_____

_____

32. Sticky Fingers

Dennis didn't plan to steal the CD when he walked into the music store. He had planned to buy the newest CD by his favorite rock group. He saw that it cost several dollars more than he had brought with him. He hid the CD under his jacket.

Dennis looked around the store to see if there were any security cameras. He . . .

_____

_____

_____

_____

_____

_____

_____

_____

_____

33.

Help!

When Roman got home, he discovered that he did not have his house key with him. Both the front door and the back door were locked. He picked up a crowbar from a pile of his Dad's tools in the backyard and tried to pry a window open. The window snapped open so suddenly that it smashed back against the wall, glass shattered all over, and a large piece hit Roman's arm and cut it badly.

"Help!" screamed Roman, as he tried to stop the bleeding with the shirt he was wearing. He . . .

_____

_____

_____

_____

_____

_____

_____

_____

34. A Dilemma

When Maureen walked into a supermarket to buy a snack, she saw a man who appeared to be shoplifting. He was slipping several packages of food into his coat pocket. The man looked old and poor and probably had no money. He might even have been living on the streets.

Maureen knew she should report shoplifting, but should she report this poor man? She . . .

_____

_____

_____

_____

_____

_____

_____

_____

_____

_____

35.　Leave Me Alone

Sam was sick of having other boys at school bully him if he did not give them money. Several boys would surround him in the bathroom or the gym, where it was difficult for a teacher to see what was happening. Sam knew it was wrong not to report these boys, but he was afraid they would get back at him if he did. Still, he was fed up with the treatment.

Finally, Sam had a plan. He . . .

_____

_____

_____

_____

_____

_____

_____

_____

_____

_____

36. I Can See Clearly Now

Ann was upset that the eye doctor had told her she needed to wear glasses. She would look awful in glasses! Her mother helped her pick some very pretty, stylish frames, but she still didn't like the idea. People might make fun of how she looked!

The first day Ann had the glasses, she was surprised to see how clear everything looked on the chalkboard. She . . .

_____

_____

_____

_____

_____

_____

_____

_____

_____

_____

37. To Stay or Not to Stay?

Janice was often asked to stay home in the evening when her parents worked late. Her grandmother lived with the family and might need Janice's help. Janice was glad to help but wanted time with her friends, too. She loved her grandmother, but she didn't want to feel "tied down."

One evening when Janice and her grandmother were home alone, Janice got a phone call inviting her to a party just down the block. She . . .

_____

_____

_____

_____

_____

_____

_____

_____

_____

38. Which College, Rachel?

Rachel wanted to go to college many miles from her home and live in the college housing. She knew it was a good college. It had all the classes she wanted to take, and several of her friends were going there. Her parents could afford to send her there and had asked her to select her own college. She knew that her grades were good and that she would be admitted there.

After Rachel's father had told her to make her own choice, he shocked her with an announcement. He . . .

_____

_____

_____

_____

_____

_____

_____

_____

_____

39. What's the Solution?

Matt's summer job was so boring! He worked in an office filing papers and filling orders. The people he worked with were very nice, but the work was so dull! He needed the spending money but began to wonder if it was worth it—he could be at the beach with his friends.

Finally, Matt had an idea that might be a solution. He . . .

_____

_____

_____

_____

_____

_____

_____

_____

_____

_____

_____

40. Too Many Absences

Celeste missed school a day or two a week. She hated school and was determined to miss it as often as possible. If she even hinted that she felt ill, her mother let her stay home and watch television. Some of her friends were jealous. Their parents accepted few excuses for missing school.

One afternoon a school counselor phoned Celeste at home and, in a supportive way, asked her what the school could do to encourage her to attend more often. Celeste . . .

_____

_____

_____

_____

_____

_____

_____

_____

_____

_____

41. Missing Money

Peter found a notebook at his desk when he got to his math class one morning. He looked inside at the pages to see if he could tell to whom it belonged. He looked in the plastic pencil case on the notebook rings to see if he could find an identification card, but he could not. He took the notebook to the teacher.

Minutes later, a girl from an earlier class came in and claimed the notebook, looked inside, and said that ten dollars was missing from the pencil case. Peter . . .

_____

_____

_____

_____

_____

_____

_____

_____

_____

42. A Talented Musician

Olivia was very quiet and shy, but she did love being in the school orchestra. She usually played the violin, but the teacher, Ms. West, knew that she played *five* other instruments! Olivia had studied music since she was very young. She was also talented at playing the saxophone, the flute, the clarinet, the guitar, and the piano. Most of the other students did not know that Olivia was such a skilled musician!

For the holiday program, Ms. West made an interesting proposal to Olivia. She . . .

_____

_____

_____

_____

_____

_____

_____

_____

_____

43. Expecting Perfection

At the school's open house meeting, Anita's father asked her history teacher how well she was doing in the class. The teacher replied that Anita was a wonderful student and had a record of many A's and one B at that point in the school year. Her father asked about the one B. The teacher smiled and said that Anita was a terrific student and there was nothing to worry about.

Standing with her father, Anita suddenly blurted out, "Why do you always expect me to be perfect, Dad?" She . . .

_____

_____

_____

_____

_____

_____

_____

_____

44. Dress Dispute

Monica picked a beautiful blue silk dress to wear to the school dance. She used most of the money she had saved from her after-school job to buy it. She took it home and tried it on to show to her mother and sister, who both thought it looked terrific on her. Then she showed it to her father, who surprised her when he exclaimed that it was too form-fitting and revealing for her to wear out of the house.

Monica told her father that he was too old-fashioned and that she intended to wear the dress to the dance. She . . .

_____

_____

_____

_____

_____

_____

_____

_____

_____

45. A Difficult Choice

Father Joseph was the most loved and the bravest priest that St. Anne's Church had ever had. The priest said Mass and performed all the usual rituals, but he also served the poor. He made his church a sanctuary for immigrants and a home for men and women who lived on the streets. He tried to teach the church members that they must truly serve all people. Father Joseph helped everyone—even immigrants who were in the country illegally.

Immigration officials came to warn Father Joseph that he might be arrested if he continued to shelter illegal immigrants. Father Joseph . . .

_____

_____

_____

_____

_____

_____

_____

_____

46. Fire!

The weather was unusually hot and dry—temperatures soared to well over 100 degrees. Several fires were started by arsonists. Jim's family saw one of the fires just two blocks from their own home. Jim's parents grabbed important family papers and photos, and Jim grabbed his little sister. Together they all ran to the family car.

As Jim's father drove them all away from the area, Jim turned back and saw that sparks had hit their roof and a small fire had already started! He . . .

_____

_____

_____

_____

_____

_____

_____

_____

_____

47.   Be Prepared

Larry dreaded having to stand in front of the class to give his report. Aside from being nervous about how well he would do on the assignment, he was very self-conscious because he was overweight. Other students often teased him about it. He gathered his papers and illustrations and placed them on the table in front of the class.

He thought he was prepared for anything, but then he heard a boy whisper very loudly, "Hey! It's Fatso!" He . . .

_____

_____

_____

_____

_____

_____

_____

_____

_____

48. Why Clean?

Beth got upset every time her mother told her to clean her room. It was *her* room, and she felt she should be able to leave her belongings arranged as she wanted them. She kept food and drinks out of the room, so why did a few piles of clothes, odd stacks of papers, and a little dust bother her mother so much? What a silly thing to argue about!

One afternoon Beth's mother got very angry and told Beth she would be grounded for a month if she didn't clean her room. Beth . . .

_____

_____

_____

_____

_____

_____

_____

_____

_____

_____

49.   No Smoking

Arturo and his friends sat down at a table in their favorite restaurant. A man at the next table was smoking cigarettes, and the smoke was making Arturo cough. Couldn't the man see the sign on the wall that said, "NO SMOKING"? Why hadn't the restaurant manager spoken to him?

Determined to be firm but polite, Arturo decided to speak to the man himself. He . . .

_____

_____

_____

_____

_____

_____

_____

_____

_____

_____

50. Sympathy for Alexis

Alexis had been absent from school for several days. Just before she returned, the teacher told the class that she had been absent because her mother had died of cancer. She mentioned that it would be thoughtful for students to express their sympathy, but that they should avoid asking Alexis to talk about it if she did not want to. The class was silent for a moment, and then various students began to talk about how sad Alexis must feel.

When Alexis returned to school the next day, her friend Mary went up to her and hugged her. She . . .

_____

_____

_____

_____

_____

_____

_____

_____

_____

51. Lucky Omar

Omar burst into class one morning, excited and laughing. Since he was usually rather quiet, the class was surprised. Omar announced that his father had won several million dollars in the state lottery two days earlier! The class thought he was playing a trick on them and started to tease him about his story.

Omar said he could prove it to the class and pulled a newspaper out of his notebook. He . . .

_____

_____

_____

_____

_____

_____

_____

_____

_____

52.   Moving Up

Jackie had the highest grade in English, but she didn't like the class. Too many of the kids were loud and disruptive, and the teacher had to spend too much time dealing with their poor behavior. Jackie was surprised when the teacher asked *her* to stay after class for a chat! It turned out that the teacher wanted to invite her to transfer to her honors English class, where she felt Jackie could work well and the behavior was much better.

Jackie was thrilled! She . . .

_____

_____

_____

_____

_____

_____

_____

_____

_____

53. Weapon Ban

When Alan looked into Victor's open backpack, he thought he saw a gun wedged between two books. His heart began to pound as he wondered what to do. Victor was a great guy who would never hurt anyone! But signs posted around the school read, "If you see a weapon, report it, and save a life."

Alan decided he'd better go right to the assistant principal. He . . .

_____

_____

_____

_____

_____

_____

_____

_____

_____

54. Look Who's Talking!

Sabrina opened her mouth wide so that her friends could see the new stud in her tongue. A few thought it was cool, but others said it was creepy! Liz, who had five earrings in her left ear and tattoos on both arms, announced that Sabrina just wanted attention. Sabrina laughed loudly and pointed at Liz's tattoos.

Then both girls glared at each other. Sabrina . . .

_____

_____

_____

_____

_____

_____

_____

_____

_____

_____

55. A Dangerous Escape

Binh wrote a story for the school newspaper that caught everyone's attention. In the story he told of his family's long and dangerous escape from Vietnam after the war there. The group he was in had lived in filthy refugee camps where they had nearly starved, and the last of their money had been stolen. After a long and dangerous boat trip to Malaysia, they were able to board a plane that took them to Thailand and then to the United States.

In class, students asked Binh to tell them more about his family's escape. He . . .

_____

_____

_____

_____

_____

_____

_____

_____

_____

_____

56. Protecting Ray

Ray had been coming to school for weeks with black-and-blue marks on his arms. He said he got the marks from falling off his bike or bumping into things. Finally, Ray admitted to his closest friend, Ed, that his father had been beating him. He showed Ed a huge bruise on his back.

Ed was upset and wanted Ray to report the abuse to a counselor or a teacher. He . . .

_____

_____

_____

_____

_____

_____

_____

_____

_____

_____

57. Where's Mom?

Denise usually got home from school at 3:30 in the afternoon. Her mother always walked in from work at exactly 5:30. If she was going to stop to do some errands, she always phoned Denise to tell her when she'd be home. In turn, Denise always phoned her mom if she planned to stay late at a friend's house.

One evening, Denise's mother did not phone, and at 6:15 she was still not home. Denise . . .

_____

_____

_____

_____

_____

_____

_____

_____

_____

58.

A Bad Break

When Caroline sat down at the dinner table, her parents seemed uneasy. As they began the meal, Caroline's father told her and her younger sister, Diane, that he and her mother had decided to get a divorce. He began to explain the decision, but Diane began to cry. Caroline got up and ran to her room and slammed the door.

Caroline's father came into her room and asked if they could talk. Caroline . . .

_____

_____

_____

_____

_____

_____

_____

_____

_____

_____

59.   Intruder!

Valerie was home alone when she heard strange noises on the front porch. She peeked out a window and saw a man trying to pry open the front door! Valerie was very scared, but she tried not to panic. She knew she had to think straight and get help right away.

Valerie ran to the kitchen and grabbed the phone. She . . .

_____

_____

_____

_____

_____

_____

_____

_____

_____

60. Smart Wayne

Sometimes Wayne brought his homework to class on time, and sometimes he didn't. One afternoon his teacher asked him why he did not bring in every assignment. At first Wayne mumbled something about forgetting his papers. Then he blurted out, "I guess I'm just stupid, like my father always says!"

Surprised, the teacher replied that she found Wayne to be very smart, and that the papers he did were very well written. Wayne . . .

_____

_____

_____

_____

_____

_____

_____

_____

_____

_____

61.   Laura's Role

Laura had a serious muscular disease and used a wheelchair. An aide accompanied her to classes to help her with some tasks, but Laura could propel her chair around the room herself and asked students for help when she needed it. When the class decided to put on a play, Laura wanted to have a role. "And don't cast me in the part of a girl in a wheelchair," she said.

The class and the teacher figured out what to do. They . . .

_____

_____

_____

_____

_____

_____

_____

_____

_____

62.

Missing!

Christina lived with her mother and stepfather. Her stepfather was very strict, and Christina often tried to get her mother to stand up for her. When her mother defended her stepfather, Christina talked about running away from home. Her friends got scared when they heard her talk like that.

One day, after a nasty argument with her stepfather, Christina did not return home when she was expected. She . . .

_____

_____

_____

_____

_____

_____

_____

_____

_____

_____

63. No Nuclear War!

Marianne saw films in her history class about the use of the atomic bomb on Hiroshima at the end of World War II. She read articles about the modern nuclear weapons that so many nations have. She became very frightened. Articles in the newspapers about the construction of new weapons didn't help.

Marianne decided to ask her teacher and classmates if they could all discuss things students might do to learn about and help prevent nuclear war. She . . .

_____

_____

_____

_____

_____

_____

_____

_____

_____

64.   Exhausted

Desmond could scarcely stay awake in class. He worked in a market after school and had to help take care of his two little brothers when he got home. His parents both worked long, hard hours at their jobs and needed his help. He was exhausted by the time he got to class each morning.

As class started one morning, Desmond's teacher thought he looked tired and ill and asked him if he needed to go see the school nurse. Desmond . . .

_____

_____

_____

_____

_____

_____

_____

_____

_____

_____

65. Festival Time

When Jonathon and Rajeev headed for the international festival downtown, they were afraid it might consist of boring, museum-like exhibits. But as soon as they arrived, they were amazed by the exotic sights, smells, and sounds that greeted them. "I had no idea there were people from so many different cultures in our city!" Rajeev exclaimed.

First, the boys watched Greek dancers and ate Thai food. Then . . .

_____

_____

_____

_____

_____

_____

_____

_____

_____

66.　Who Are You?

Ernest and Eugene were twins. They were serious students, but sometimes they liked to play tricks on their teachers and friends. They had the same teacher for history but at different hours. One morning, Ernest went to Eugene's history class and Eugene went to Ernest's math class.

Ernest sat down in Eugene's seat in history and got out the day's lesson. He . . .

_____

_____

_____

_____

_____

_____

_____

_____

_____

67. Transferred!

Kyle had already been punished for writing all over his desk in several classes. Then he was caught spray-painting graffiti on the school-building walls. He really made a mess! The principal called a meeting with Kyle, his school counselor, and his parents.

When the principal announced that Kyle would be transferred to another school for this offense, Kyle's father objected. He . . .

_____

_____

_____

_____

_____

_____

_____

_____

_____

_____

68. Angry Words

Jim took the summons paper and went to talk to his counselor about his science class, where he was not doing well. "That teacher is so unfair," Jim yelled. "I'd kill him if I could!" he exclaimed. The counselor looked startled and asked Jim if he knew that what he had just said could get him arrested and expelled from the school.

Jim was terrified! He . . .

_____

_____

_____

_____

_____

_____

_____

_____

_____

69. Love of Music

Claire was excited about going off to college in the fall. Her father asked her to concentrate on earning high grades so that she could qualify for law school and then join his law firm. The two of them had discussed this possibility before, but now Claire told her father she had decided to major in music, a subject she loved and did well in. Her father banged his fist down on the table and announced that he would not pay college costs for such a "useless" field of study!

Claire was so stunned she could not speak for a moment. She . . .

_____

_____

_____

_____

_____

_____

_____

_____

_____

_____

70.   Go, Steven!

Steven loved sports, but he wasn't very skilled in any game. When he tried to make a basket or catch a softball, he usually messed up. He knew he'd never be a star, but he did the best he could. Luckily, his classmates cheered him on instead of laughing at him.

One day, Steven went up to bat, determined to hit a home run. He . . .

_____

_____

_____

_____

_____

_____

_____

_____

_____

_____

71.   Greg! Your Hair!

Greg came to school one morning with a strange new hairstyle. He had shaved his head on one side and dyed the hair on the other side bright orange. He got plenty of stares and comments. One boy told him he looked like a freak!

Greg wanted to hit the boy, but he knew that a fight could mean suspension from school. He . . .

_____

_____

_____

_____

_____

_____

_____

_____

_____

_____

72. Caught by Guard

Sergio and his friends liked to go to rock concerts, but they were so expensive! This was no problem when groups appeared at the outdoor theater, as no one seemed to mind when kids sat far behind the last seats on a grassy hill behind the theater. Sergio and his friends did that from time to time, and they could hear the music quite well. One evening Sergio saw that the last row of seats in the theater were empty, so he slid down the hill and stepped over the low wall at the back of the theater.

Just as Sergio got to a seat in the last row, a uniformed guard he had not noticed grabbed him by the arm. Sergio . . .

_____

_____

_____

_____

_____

_____

_____

_____

_____

73. You're Late!

Elena had told her parents she would be home by 10:00 P.M., but it was 11:15 when she looked at her watch! She and her friends were having so much fun at the party she hadn't noticed the time. She phoned her parents, told them what had happened, and then went straight home. She hoped they would not be too angry.

When she walked in the front door, Elena could see that her father was waiting for her and looked upset. She . . .

_____

_____

_____

_____

_____

_____

_____

_____

_____

74.   Ouch!

Holly always enjoyed baby-sitting for eight-year-old Brooke. Brooke was never any trouble! But one day, Brooke had an accident on her bicycle. She was racing down a hill at top speed when she hit a bump in the pavement. After tumbling onto the concrete, Brooke picked herself up and broke into sobs. Her arm hurt very badly when she tried to move it.

When Holly looked at Brooke's arm, she was sure it was broken. Holly . . .

_____

_____

_____

_____

_____

_____

_____

_____

_____

_____

75. A Hair-Raising Question

Britney was nervous about returning to school wearing a wig. It didn't look bad, but Britney did not want to answer a bunch of questions about the treatment for cancer she had just completed. The medications had made all her hair fall out. Her best friends knew all about it, but not the whole eighth-grade class!

The first day back, a girl she barely knew yelled across the room, "Hey, Britney! What's up with that haircut?" Britney . . .

_____

_____

_____

_____

_____

_____

_____

_____

_____

_____

76.   We Care!

When Latrice had to go to the hospital for some minor surgery, she was almost glad for the time away from school and the conceited kids she had to see every day. So she was surprised when one close friend, along with three girls she didn't know very well, came all the way across town on the bus to visit her. Then her math teacher, Ms. Conroe, stopped by with flowers and hugs. More kids called on the phone to wish her well.

"I had no idea so many people cared about me," Latrice said to her mom. She . . .

_____

_____

_____

_____

_____

_____

_____

_____

77.   Wild Susan

Susan knew how to be a serious, mature student in the classroom, but she also knew how to have fun with her friends. In class, her behavior was perfect and her work earned top grades. In the school halls and on the P.E. field, Susan was loud and silly. At a dance, watch out! Susan was wild!

One day Susan forgot to change back into her serious self as she entered the classroom. She . . .

_____

_____

_____

_____

_____

_____

_____

_____

_____

_____

78.   Wake Up!

Mrs. Robertson noticed that Myra often fell asleep in class. At first she tapped the girl on her shoulder and asked her to sit up. Then she told Myra to stay after class one day and asked her why she was tired so frequently. At first Myra did not want to answer and just said that she felt fine.

Then Myra decided that Mrs. Robertson really cared about her, so she decided to tell her what was going on. She . . .

_____

_____

_____

_____

_____

_____

_____

_____

_____

_____

79. Speaking Freely

Antonia was confused by some of the things the teacher asked her English class to do. She was a newly arrived immigrant and already spoke English well. Her confusion was with the type of work the teacher assigned. The teacher was always asking students their opinion of the stories they read and what they thought of ideas that were presented. In Antonia's home country, they had just recited facts and memorized lines.

The teacher saw Antonia's confusion and decided to speak to her. She . . .

_____

_____

_____

_____

_____

_____

_____

_____

_____

80. New Thoughts About Camp

Jessica really hated summer camp! Why had her parents sent her to such a place? The food was awful, the kids were not very friendly to her, and the hikes were long and hard. The only thing she really liked was the horseback riding.

One day, something happened that made Jessica feel that the camp was not so bad after all. She . . .

_____

_____

_____

_____

_____

_____

_____

_____

_____

81.   Haneefa's Culture

Haneefa was a new student at school. Her family had recently come to the United States from India. Other girls asked her about the clothes she wore, her accent, and why she wore a jewel in her nose! Haneefa could tell that the questions were friendly. She told her new classmates a great deal about her country and her culture.

Haneefa's new friends were surprised to hear that she could speak five languages! She . . .

_____

_____

_____

_____

_____

_____

_____

_____

_____

_____

82.   I Am Me!

Kurt was the third boy from his family to attend the same junior high school. He was often uncomfortable because the teachers all knew his two older brothers, who had been straight-A students. Kurt usually earned C's and did not like to be reminded to work as hard as his brothers had. He was not one of his brothers—he was Kurt!

One day in English class, Kurt even wrote a paper about being seen as himself, not as someone's little brother. He . . .

_____

_____

_____

_____

_____

_____

_____

_____

_____

83. Braces

The day Jeffrey got braces on his teeth, he didn't want to go back to school. Sure, lots of kids had them, but they were so ugly! Someone would call him names or tease him. He was sure everyone would stare at him.

Back in school, Jeffrey tried to keep his mouth closed. He . . .

_____

_____

_____

_____

_____

_____

_____

_____

_____

_____

84. Playing Hooky

Mrs. Vogel noticed that Ramon and Derek were both absent from her science class quite often, and on the same days. When she asked the boys about it, they had notes that said they had been sick. She called the parents and found out that they had no idea the boys had been absent frequently. The notes were forged. The boys had pretended to leave for school, but they went back home after they knew their parents had gone to work.

At home that night, Ramon's father demanded to know what was going on. Ramon . . .

_____

_____

_____

_____

_____

_____

_____

_____

_____

85.   I Won't Move!

Scott was angry when his parents told him they were going to move to a new house. The house was only a few miles away, but moving would mean changing schools. He would not be in the same classes or on the same teams with his friends. Besides, Scott liked the old house and neighborhood.

Scott yelled at his parents that he simply was not going to move! He . . .

_____

_____

_____

_____

_____

_____

_____

_____

_____

_____

86.   Robbed!

When Felicia and her family got home from a movie late one evening, it was clear that their house had been robbed. Furniture was overturned. Drawers and closets had been emptied, and things were thrown all over the place. The house was a complete mess!

Felicia's father grabbed the phone and called the police. He . . .

_____

_____

_____

_____

_____

_____

_____

_____

_____

_____

87. Keisha's Chores

Every Saturday, Keisha was supposed to help with the housecleaning chores while her mother was at work. Keisha usually washed the dishes, vacuumed the rugs, and cleaned the bathroom. But one Saturday, Keisha decided to go to the mall with her friends instead of doing her chores. The dirty dishes were left in the sink. The rugs did not get vacuumed. The bathroom did not get cleaned.

When Keisha's mother got home, she was furious. She . . .

_____

_____

_____

_____

_____

_____

_____

_____

_____

_____

88. Inside Out

Although there was no official dress code in force, Owen was sent to the office by his math teacher for wearing inappropriate clothing. His black T-shirt was plain on front, but it had an alcohol advertisement printed on the back. The principal agreed that the shirt was inappropriate for school and asked Owen to turn his shirt inside out.

"My father allows me to wear this shirt, and the school should, too!" Owen shouted. The principal . . .

_____

_____

_____

_____

_____

_____

_____

_____

_____

_____

89. A National Treasure

Andrew had never been to a national park before, so seeing it for the first time was exciting. The trees were so tall! Buffalo, deer, and moose roamed everywhere. Everything was so peaceful and beautiful compared to the noise and dirt of the city.

Andrew decided to join a hike with a park ranger so he could learn about his new surroundings. He . . .

_____

_____

_____

_____

_____

_____

_____

_____

_____

_____

90. Surprise!

Isabel could not understand why her two closest friends had not mentioned her birthday. The three girls always exchanged birthday gifts and cards and hugs. But today, when Isabel turned fifteen, neither friend had said a thing! Isabel walked into her house wondering why they had forgotten.

As she opened the front door, Isabel heard at least a dozen voices yell, "Surprise!" She . . .

_____

_____

_____

_____

_____

_____

_____

_____

_____

91. A Tough Decision

Salvador was grateful to his friend Russell for getting him a job at the supermarket after school. Russell had said it was a great place to work, and it was. However, after just a few days on the job, Salvador noticed that Russell took food from the shelves for his snacks and did not pay for what he took. Salvador wondered if he should report his friend for stealing, the friend who had gotten him the job.

Salvador could not decide what to do. He . . .

_____

_____

_____

_____

_____

_____

_____

_____

_____

_____

92. First-Day Ticket

The first day Adrienne had her driver's license, she got a traffic ticket! To celebrate her new license, Adrienne's father had allowed her to borrow his car and drive with several friends to a movie theater. They had not noticed a two-hour-only parking sign and had returned after nearly three hours to find a ticket on the windshield. It would cost twenty-two dollars!

Adrienne knew a parking ticket was not as serious as a ticket for something dangerous, like speeding, but she was embarrassed to tell her father. She . . .

_____

_____

_____

_____

_____

_____

_____

_____

_____

93. To Speak or Not to Speak

Byron stayed at his grandparents' house as often as he could. That way, he didn't have to hear his parents argue all the time, or get hit whenever his father was mad at him. It was more comfortable to do his schoolwork and have friends over at Grandma's, too. He and his friends loved his grandma's warm greetings and his grandpa's jokes.

When his father asked him why he stayed at his grandparents' so often, Byron wasn't sure what to say. He . . .

_____

_____

_____

_____

_____

_____

_____

_____

_____

94. Freedom of Expression

Nikki wrote several articles for the school newspaper in which she expressed thoughtful opinions on world events. The journalism teacher promised to print them, but the principal said the articles could not appear. She said the school paper was for school news only. Nikki felt the principal was just afraid of free expression of ideas and opinions.

Nikki decided to write a new article for the school paper arguing for freedom of expression for students. She . . .

_____

_____

_____

_____

_____

_____

_____

_____

_____

95.   Keeping Fido

A dog followed David all the way home from the playground one afternoon. It had no collar or license. It was a friendly mutt, and David begged his parents to let him keep it if no owner turned up. His parents weren't sure what to do, but they let David keep the dog in the backyard for that night.

The next morning the doorbell rang. David . . .

_____

_____

_____

_____

_____

_____

_____

_____

_____

_____

96. A Day at the Beach

Linda decided to go to the beach for the afternoon. She played volleyball with some friends and then went wading in the ocean. She watched some little children, busy with their pails and shovels, building a sand castle. After sunbathing for a while, Linda decided to get a snack.

Linda walked over to the area that had the food stands, shops, and a roller coaster. She . . .

_____

_____

_____

_____

_____

_____

_____

_____

_____

_____

97. Last-Minute Adam

Mrs. Tanaka had been right when she gave the assignment—leaving a long report to write until the night before it was due was foolish! Adam had rushed to the library that afternoon to get the books he needed. He saw that there was a great deal of material to cover. He took notes and began to write as quickly as he could.

At two o'clock in the morning, Adam still wasn't finished writing. He . . .

_____

_____

_____

_____

_____

_____

_____

_____

_____

_____

98.   Tony Is Toni!

Josh decided to try out for the basketball team that was going to compete in a charity game against the faculty. Friends warned him that the captain of the team, Tony, was very demanding and skilled, and only let the best players onto the court. Josh bragged that he was a great player and would have no problem. Just then, Tony showed up to start the practice for tryouts. Josh was shocked—Tony was *Toni!*

"A *girl* runs this team?" exclaimed Josh. He . . .

_____

_____

_____

_____

_____

_____

_____

_____

_____

_____

99.   Circus Magic

Enrique had never seen a circus before, so when it came to town he was anxious to see it. He watched the men set up the tents and tend the animals. He peeked through an opening in a tent and saw the trapeze artists rehearsing. He followed a line of clowns as they paraded around, advertising the circus.

The day of the first performance, Enrique was one of the first people in line to buy a ticket. He . . .

_____

_____

_____

_____

_____

_____

_____

_____

_____

_____

_____

100. A Frightening Fall

It was a sunny, breezy Saturday and a perfect day to spend by the pool with family. Paul played and splashed with his cousins while the adults sipped drinks and sat in the shade. Suddenly, three-year-old Becky slipped and fell into the deep end of the pool. In seconds, Becky was coughing and struggling in the water!

Paul was closest, and without a second thought he dived into the pool. He . . .

_____

_____

_____

_____

_____

_____

_____

_____

_____